IT *IS* WHETHER YOU WIN OR LOSE *AND* HOW YOU PLAY THE GAME

By: Lance Dearborn

Dedication

Live and help live.
—Lamar Moody

Born on a farm in rural Florida in 1929, Lamar Moody learned to read at night by the light of a kerosene lantern. Moody wanted a different kind of life, one lived away from the family farm, and that meant creating a plan—one that included college— for the life he wanted. He became valedictorian of his high school class and went on to receive four degrees, finishing with a doctorate in educational leadership. He devoted his entire life to helping young people achieve their dreams. Lamar was my father-in-law and an incredible inspiration to me.

Intention

A dream is just a dream. A goal is a dream with a plan and a deadline. —Harvey Mackay

I have written this book for every person who wants something different—something more—from life and is willing to sacrifice and work hard to achieve it. This book is my life's story and my best practices guide to help others plot a course toward a better future.

This book is especially written for young men and women who are just now beginning to make impactful, life-altering decisions. Over three million people graduate high school each year, and one million more drop out of school. This means that annually about four million people need a plan! A plan—a map—that both defines life success and provides a list of the steps necessary to reach an intended destination. With a plan, and the willingness to work hard and sacrifice, victory in life is within reach.

This book is specifically written to my

daughter, Lindsey Dearborn, as she departs the security of our home and ventures into the greatness the world has to offer her. Lindsey has grown into a responsible, hard-working, and delightful person. Greatness is within her reach, and I am confident she will take the steps necessary to achieve it.

In my high school years, I made significant mistakes because I did not plan for success. I had no plan at all. Day after day, I repeated the same actions which became habits. This pattern of consistent complacency led to bad decisions and put my life on the path of failure. I was fortunate enough to meet mentors and other leaders whose life examples encouraged me to begin considering my own future, my own success, and I created a new path for myself, one that has led me to achieve success. Within this book, I share my story. I share my life. I share what I believe is my purpose.

In my judgment, personal winning is not enough. We have a responsibility to ourselves and our family to win at life. We also have a responsibility to make the world a better place because we were here.

CONTENTS

Dedication v

Intention vi

Introduction 1

Part One: On Life 9

Winning and Helping Others Succeed Are Equally
Important 10

Nothing Good Happens Without a Plan 12

Manage Your Life 15

Opportunity Can Be a Game Changer 17

Believe to Achieve 20

Own the Past, but Don't Live There 22

Pay It Forward 24

Faith Matters: Take Time to Contemplate God's
Existence and Presence 27

Family Is First 30

Control the Controllable 32

Life Is Good 34

Love Yourself and Recognize Reality 35

Quick Hitters for Life 37

Part Two: On Business 44

Start Your Day Early 45

Never Stop Improving Yourself 47

Image Is Important 49

Organize, Organize, Organize 52

Control Your Emotions 54

Trust but Verify 56

Teamwork 59

Deal with Reality (It Is What It Is) 62

I'm the Hardest Working 84-Year-Old You'll Ever Meet 64

Complaining Is for Losers; Deal with It or Quit 67

If You're Going to Do Something, Do It Well 68

Freight on the Dock 70

Let Others Gossip for You 72

How You Leave a Relationship Is as Important as How You Enter It 74

When We Lose It's My Fault; When We Win It's Their Credit 76

Grow Wisely 78

Good Times Aren't Here Forever; Plan for Lean Times 80

Time Is a Non-Renewable Resource; Use It Wisely 83

Short-Term Solutions Don't Solve Long-Term Problems 85

Live Life to Win; Don't be Afraid of Losing 87

Make the Lives of Others Easier by Working for Their Benefit 91

Saying No Is Taking the Easy Way Out 94

Every Yard Has Bugs 96

Loyalty Is a Two-Way Street 98

Organizational Circles 101

Quickly Answer Your Emails, Voicemails, and Texts 102

Fire People in Person 103

If You Swim to Shore, Walk onto Land 105

Success Does Not Happen by Luck 107

Quick Hitters for Business 108

Improve Every Situation because You Are a Part

of It...112

A Challenge: Be a Rock Not a Feather...................114

Notes...116

Introduction

At age eight, I was Paola Little League's T-ball Triple Crown winner. That spring, I had the most home runs, best batting average, and the most runs batted in (RBI). I was the best player on the team. We practiced and played our games in the outfield of the older kids' field, and each time we played, the coach set up our tee—an old construction cone—and temporary bases. There was no outfield fence. If a batter managed to hit a ball past the outfielders, he could easily run the bases and score a run. The field's quality was unimportant to me. I simply wanted to play; I wanted to be the best. In my eight-year-old mind, I was the next Pete Rose and on my way to playing professional baseball.

Back then, baseball was everything to me. My home, a trailer in a park a few minutes away, was not exactly luxurious. No trailer park in Sanford, Florida in the '70s could make that claim. But it was there, as I started playing baseball, that I began to learn valuable life lessons, lessons taught through sports, lessons that I use in life and business today.

At eight I wanted to be a professional baseball player, but by 11 or 12 I wasn't the best player anymore, and I never was again. My dream of professional sports was just that, a dream. In a sport where a fraction of a second matters, I knew by middle school that I wouldn't play beyond little league. Even though my baseball dream was not going to happen, I wanted more from life. I couldn't describe what 'more' was fully at that age, but I knew that I didn't want to live in a trailer park. I knew that I wanted to go out to dinner without having to spend rent money. I wanted to take my future family on vacations. I didn't want to base every decision on not having enough money.

From Sanford, we moved to another trailer park, this one in Bithlo, Florida. Let me say this, money makes life easier, but it does not create happiness. My family life was poor but happy. My mom and dad are models of unconditional love. They love one another and their children wholeheartedly. My dad, who has a pure heart and a constant desire to help others and do the right thing for everyone, coached my baseball team. My mom was involved in all of our activities. She is one of the smartest and most hard-working people I have ever known. Our family did a lot together, but every decision we made centered around a lack of financial resources. Supporting a growing family of three, then four, then five children was a constant struggle. This struggle shaped my view of the world. I wanted the happiness of our family with the freedom money provides.

I grew up with an older brother, Eric, and a younger sister, Cathy. Only four years separated the three of us. When I was 10, Kevin, my youngest brother, was born. Michelle, my youngest sister, arrived when I was 14. We were a fairly normal family; sometimes we argued and sometimes we got along well. Today I look forward to the time we spend together as a family whether that time is in person or over the phone.

When I was eight, my parents asked me to ride my bike to the convenience store located about a mile away to buy bread for dinner. The route to the store was familiar to me; it was a trip I had made dozens of times before. I made the trip there easily, purchased the bread, and started pedaling toward home. About a block away from our trailer, I realized the bottom of the bag had been hitting against my front tire spokes. A gaping hole had allowed all but two slices of bread to escape.

Behind me, along my path, dirty slices of bread littered the ground. Every piece was ruined. I started crying as hard as any eight-year-old could cry. My parents had given me a dollar to buy bread, and I had let them down. I did not know if they had another dollar or not. Shamefully, I walked into our trailer with the tattered bag in my hands. With tears rolling down my face, I explained what happened and told them how sorry I was.

What I remember most is the look of understanding and love on their faces. "That's okay," they said. "It was just a mistake." From that moment forward, I truly understood the meaning of unconditional love. They also trusted me enough to give me another dollar, and I returned to the store, bought a second loaf of bread, and rode it home with the care of someone clutching a million dollar lottery ticket.

Right before I entered middle school, we moved again. My parents bought a house with a pool in an affluent area. This change was a huge step for our family, and I have great respect for my parents for moving our family into a better neighborhood.

Attending an affluent school brought different struggles. Like any other preteen, I wanted to fit into the culture. I wanted to be like the rich kids, but we were as far from rich as could possibly be. I stayed focused on getting good grades and was glad when the time came to move on to high school.

Unfortunately, high school wasn't an improvement for me. I still didn't fit in. Looking back over those years now, I know I'm the one to blame. I didn't make an effort to find a home or group in which to belong there. I allowed myself to feel outside of the mainstream. It was my responsibility to connect with other students and organizations at school, and I failed.

Just before I turned 16, I applied for a job as a dishwasher at Red Lobster. The manager told me that he couldn't accept my application or discuss employment until I was 16. I took him seriously and returned on my birthday. "Can you start in an hour?" he asked. I went home to change and began working that day. Within three months, I became kitchen manager.

At best, high school was uninteresting. My job at Red Lobster became my focus. Instead of remaining a high-performing student, one who consistently made A's and B's, my grades fell. I worked almost every night until ten or eleven o'clock, which made keeping up with homework and studying for tests more difficult. I remember thinking that school was pointless. In those days, I was happier at work. My sense of self, my identity, was developing at Red Lobster. I belonged at work and not at school. I didn't have a group of close friends at school, a sports team, or club in which to belong. At the start of my senior year, I quit. It is a decision I have regretted every day since.

Instead of overcoming a demanding situation, I gave up. I failed, and the feeling of failure has stuck with me throughout my life. From the moment I quit until today, I have made it a personal priority to fulfill the commitments I make to myself and others. This event, like my young childhood, shaped my worldview.

After quitting high school, besides work, I spent the next few years avoiding real responsibilities. My routine became sleeping late into the morning and hanging out with friends. I could do whatever I wanted, and I refused to allow life's demands to intrude. Life was fun. What I didn't realize in the late '80s was that life can and should be about having a good time, but delayed gratification offers a better reward. Fun is earned after you take care of your responsibilities, and responsibility itself gives a sense of purpose and pride that makes life meaningful. Believe it or not, responsibility can be fun.

Around the time I turned 20, the reality of my situation began to intrude in my thoughts, and I found myself often considering the future. I knew seven dollars an hour wouldn't bring financial success. To reach my goal of financial independence, I knew I had to work smart. I needed a PLAN!

My first move was to leave Red Lobster for a job as a courier at Air Traffic Services in Orlando. Soon after joining the company, I was promoted and moved into the office for a position that paid a dollar more an hour. After work, I would drop into Red Lobster to visit my old friends, and I'm glad I did because during one of these visits, I met the most beautiful girl I have ever seen—before or since. Linda. She was a new cashier, and I was determined to get a date with her. Secretly, I would check her work schedule and arrange to drop by the restaurant when she was there working, though I pretended our encounters were coincidental. She was a singer who traveled with a Christian group and worked at Red Lobster when in town. I did eventually get that first date, then another, and another. Our wedding was two years later.

Meeting her, and eventually her family, I realized that I couldn't take our relationship further without stability. I knew I had to do something to create long-term success. I needed to go to college, and I had to approach college differently than high school. I had to prove to myself that I could finish what I started. After adjusting my work schedule to start my workday at four in the morning and to finish by noon, I began college at Valencia Community College and then transferred to the University of Central Florida. In three years, I graduated with a bachelor's degree in accounting then went directly into a master's degree in taxation. I had a plan and worked to execute it. It wasn't about fun. I just needed to get it done.

After receiving my graduate degree in '96, the owners of the courier company I worked for wanted to retire. I was given an offer to take an increased role with the company that would lead to full ownership. At that time, Air Traffic Services had around 10 people in the office and 30 drivers. We operated exclusively in Orlando, Florida. I had worked for five years to get a master's degree, and I had planned to take the CPA exams. Now, I had to decide whether or not to shift directions. I took the offer, and today the company is a leading last-mile delivery company providing numerous services to its customers. We have a 37-year history of successful industry relationships, 125 employees, more than 200 contract drivers, and today our reach extends with multiple distribution centers throughout the Southeast United States.

Over the years, through hard work, careful planning, and learning the value of people and teamwork, I have been able to build a company that supports hundreds of families and inspires, I hope, loyalty along with individual and collective growth. It is important to me that I provide my employees with the tools they need to be successful. I am blessed and fortunate to have gone from a high school dropout to a business owner of a relatively large and successful company.

During the years I've spent in sports and business, I've learned valuable life and leadership lessons. In *It Is Whether You Win Or Lose And How You Play The Game*, I share these lessons and take a swing at some of the top business and leadership practices that have contributed to my life success. In this book, I share how to play to win and help others in the process.

Part One: On Life

Winning and Helping Others Succeed Are Equally Important

I cringe each time I hear someone say, "It's not whether you win or lose, but how you play the game." It is a ridiculous statement. Its meaning implies that you cannot do both.

Of course you want to win. Why else play?

Winning absolutely matters. It always matters. If you go to any T-ball game in the spring, there is no scoreboard. The game is intended to teach the players the fundamentals of baseball and make the game fun. In reality, the score doesn't matter. There is not supposed to be a winner and a loser. However, every parent is keeping score. Everyone knows who won and who lost. Even in a T-ball game, winning matters.

In life, winning matters most. Each individual wins by reaching the dreams and goals set for his or her life. I've met many people, too many people, who don't win, who don't reach their dreams. Often, their lack of success is not because of uncontrollable events but because they fail to plan. They fail to define success, and they fail to plan for success.

The problem is that the saying "It's not whether

you win or lose, but how you play the game" implies that if you win, you didn't win by making right or moral choices. Both winning and helping others are equally important. You don't win in life by knocking other people down.

You don't become a successful person by leaving others out.

Success is important, yes, but succeeding while helping others is equally important. In business, there's an undercurrent of "good guys finish last" that suggests it's important to do whatever it takes to get ahead, even if that means preventing others from succeeding along the way. This mindset isn't true at all. You can be successful while helping others achieve success alongside you. In fact, you can be more successful by helping others.

I challenge myself, my employees, and I challenge you to make a positive difference in the lives of the people you touch. Some people you may encounter for a very short time—for example, when a delivery person makes a delivery, they see a person for 30 seconds—maybe the positive difference is just a smile that day. At other times, perhaps with the individuals we see on a daily basis, we can make a positive difference over an extended period of time.

Nothing Good Happens Without a Plan

To my wife, Linda: Over 25 years ago, we made a plan for our life and our family. We have achieved a lot. We have sacrificed; we have had fun; we have enjoyed the ride. I love you.

Success isn't the right address, the perfect job, wardrobe, or car. It is found in the people we love and who love us in return—those with whom we spend our lives. Still, there's no way around this truth: work is a necessity.

A lot of time is spent at work; this makes enjoying your chosen profession critical. It is equally important to work for a purpose and with a plan, to work to improve yourself and others, to win and help others succeed at the same time.

For me, success is being able to do what I want to do: take time off to spend with family, take a vacation, travel, or coach a baseball team—and experience all of this with financial freedom. I am blessed that entrepreneurship led me to success. Air Traffic Services started out as a courier service in downtown Orlando, and over its more than 37-year history, the company has evolved into a regional last-mile industry leader. In late 2015, my team went through a rebranding process and decided to change the company's name to reflect who we are as a company today. In November that year, Air Traffic Services became FASTMILE Logistics. Today, the company's continued growth and success are due to the loyalty, hard work, and dedication of its more than 125 employees. They inspire me. A large number of my employees have been with us for more than 10 years.

As a business leader and owner, I am comfortable being in charge. I welcome the responsibility of making important final decisions. The flipside of leading is that when something goes wrong, and sometimes it does, I have to take out a mirror. If a decision goes awry, it is because I messed up.

Not everyone wants to own a business or be a business leader. Like me, you have a story and unique dreams and goals you hope to achieve. It's these dreams and goals that help us define success and frame our lives, paint a mental picture of what we hope to create for ourselves. Success to one person might be climbing Mt. Everest, another might want to run marathons, and another might aspire to great artistic endeavors. Whatever the ambition, I can assure you, practically every inspired, successful person started with one thing: a plan.

Plans make the way forward clear and direct and they provide purpose for action. Many well-intentioned people reach age 40 or 50 and wonder how they arrived where they are; they are lost. Getting lost was not intentional. They simply never intended at all. Every tomorrow was spent doing what they did yesterday. One day became the next day which became the next day and then the next year. Eventually, they arrived at a point in life and thought, *How did I get here?* They got *here* by not planning to get anywhere else.

Arriving at your intended destination in life doesn't happen by accident or luck. The only way to get there, your intended destination, is to take time to define success for you individually. Spend the time necessary to discover what you enjoy most, your strengths, your motivations, dreams, and goals. Make a list of goals and develop timelines to achieve them. Next, create a task list—include deadlines—along with a list of needs and start moving ahead. Set your goals and make plans to reach them.

A coach wouldn't dream of showing up for team practice without a plan. Every coach of every sport at every level has a plan for every practice and every game. Yet, most people never set a plan for themselves. It is often true that the same person who plans a basketball practice for a group of 10 year olds will not plan his or her life.

Remember, your life should have a plan. The chance that your exact plan will become your exact life is minimal. However, if you have a plan, you can adapt as life changes and develops.

Manage Your Life

If you want to achieve success, you need to manage your life. It is YOUR life and you are in control. You control your actions, your decisions, and ultimately, your outcome. You can't stop time, and you can't control every event. However, you can control your time, and you can control how you respond to life's events. Sometimes plans fail, but at least if you have a plan, you can adapt and change.

Success for me is to do with my life what I want to do and to make a difference in the lives of others. Simply stated, I can do what I want to do. I want to enjoy life, and I manage my life to accomplish this goal. Some people spend all of their time working. I'm not saying that is wrong; many people love to work. I enjoy work, but I don't work for the fun of work.

I work to enjoy my life outside of work. I enjoy my family. I enjoy coaching. I enjoy taking a drive on Saturday without a specific destination in mind. I enjoy taking vacations. If I worked all the time, I would never have that luxury. I could save money by doing someone else's job in my company, but why should I do that? When I die, will my only legacy be a successful company? Is this really all I want to give? No, it's not. I hope professional success comes of my life. I hope it is part of my legacy, but I also hope to offer more to the world during my time here.

Owning a company provides the flexibility of doing what I want. If I choose to leave early to coach a baseball team, I don't need to ask anyone if I can take time off. My position offers me the flexibility to make the life choices that I want to make. Others may view success in different terms. That is fine. The important factor is to define success for yourself. Determine a life destination beyond today, and manage your time and actions to reach it.

There are websites and books full of information to help emerging and seasoned leaders and aspiring professionals or entrepreneurs define and develop a life plan and create goals and tasks to reach their intended destination. We are all distracted at times, and we all face adversity. Staying on track requires us to focus and to remain committed and accountable to ourselves for the goals we plan to achieve.

Opportunity Can Be a Game Changer

To my longest friend, Matt Karash: I treasure the memories of you and me as teenagers and young adults trying to find the meaning of life and how we were going to make our way in it. You and I grew up in similar financial situations, and we have done well, my friend…we have done well.

In 1997, I was presented with the opportunity to increase my role and ultimately own Air Traffic Services. This decision would change my life forever. After working five years to finish accounting bachelor's and master's degrees and readying myself for CPA exams, I had to decide if I wanted to change my plan. Was this the right opportunity for me? Why did I work so hard at getting a master's degree if I wasn't going to use it? I knew I had a good plan, and I was executing it. I intended to leave the courier business to work for an accounting firm, and I planned to make partner. After years of college, my planned goal was within my reach. It was time to leave. I needed to leave…to move forward.

I made a decision…I was staying!

In the '90s, we were involved exclusively in rush-courier deliveries. Email was new, so a document delivery service was still a necessity for many companies, and at the same time, Orlando was exploding with outward growth.

By '97 and '98, email became the standard in quick communication. Documents were now being transferred more through email and less by courier. In response, in the late '90s, we started moving more tangible goods. By '04, at the beginning of the e-commerce boom, FASTMILE started adding a small amount of warehouse space. E-commerce didn't take off as quickly as I thought it would. I expected online shopping to quickly follow the dot-com boom, the period between '95 and '00 when entrepreneurs and investors began starting and investing money in web-based businesses like eBay, Overstock.com, and Amazon.

The boom took longer to arrive than I predicted. Still accustomed to buying products from local stores and sources, shoppers were slow to trust the products and delivery services provided by online retailers. The shift in online purchasing didn't happen in '04 or '05 or '06 or even '07, but we made a plan, adjusted as we went, and were ready when the boom did happen—nearly five years after FASTMILE's initial investment.

Today, because of my early prediction, FASTMILE enjoys a unique last-mile delivery business model and a leading position in the industry. We now serve the entire Southeast United States with a network of warehouse space and distribution centers ready to meet client needs.

Many opportunities present themselves, some big, some small. By keeping your destination in mind, you'll choose which opportunities to consider and which ones to avoid. Remember, every life, every business, every job has challenges. Decide your path and stick to it through obstacles and difficulties. Ultimately, this is the only way to reach success

.

Believe to Achieve

To my parents, Rick and Phyllis Dearborn, who have taught me so much about life and how to love. Your unconditional love of each of your children together with your acceptance of our life choices has been an example for me my entire life. I love you both.

The very core of who I am, my internal voice, is a positive one. Very few people achieve what they want in life without a positive belief that success is possible. Belief in yourself is crucial to achieving your goals.

Watching Michael Jordan play basketball in the '80s and '90s was an amazing sight. At the end of a close game, everyone knew that Bulls Coach Phil Jackson would call a play to give Jordan the ball, and Jordan knew to expect to take the winning shot. The entire Bulls team knew it. The opposition knew it. Michael won game after game by taking the shot everyone knew he would take. How could one player consistently win games? He answered this himself: "You must expect great things of yourself before you can do them."[1]

People who achieve what they want in life do so

because they are positive and believe in their ability to achieve. I believed I could achieve personal and financial success. I had confidence in myself that if I made a plan and started taking action, that I could achieve success for myself. I then wanted to share that success with those people who helped me achieve it and anyone I encountered along the way.

A plan combined with belief can take you a long way, straight to achieving your goals. Belief can help you overcome life's obstacles, bad decisions, challenging economies, and just about anything else that might emerge. As long as you believe in yourself and your plan, the remainder is only a task list. Expect to work hard. It is true that nothing worth having comes easily. To be sure, you'll grow along the way. The day you get there you'll look back and think, *That wasn't so hard.*

Own the Past, but Don't Live There

I have played men's softball for over 25 seasons. I love the competition, the camaraderie amongst friends, and the challenge of playing sports. In the early 2000s, my team was the defending league champions, and I was both the team's coach and third baseman. In the season's opening game, we played an excellent team. The opposing team came to bat first, and they scored run after run. Ground balls got past us, and poor throws kept us from getting outs. We couldn't get a play right, and the harder we tried the more errors we made. By the end of the first half of the first inning, we were behind 11-0. What a terrible way to start the season. We entered the dugout down on ourselves, wondering what had just happened.

Nothing could change what had already happened. Focusing on that 11-0 score would accomplish nothing. All we could do now was leave the previous inning behind and support one another if we wanted to score a few runs for ourselves. In the bottom of the first inning, we scored 14 runs and went on to easily win the game. We continued to win games and went on to win the league championship again that season and for the next six years in a row.

That game was a relatively meaningless softball game, but it illustrates what people can allow to happen in life. Often, a person allows a single bad event or decision to dictate the next, and on and on. Before too long, one bad event or decision leads to a bad situation.

We all make mistakes. When you make a mistake, make it a point to learn from what went wrong and then forget about it. The next time the situation arises, you will make a correct decision.

My decision to quit high school was a bad one, and it impacted me deeply. I knew that to live the life I envisioned, I needed to make changes; I needed to make a plan for success. I worked hard, both in college and at my job, and was blessed to graduate and build a thriving company. It didn't happen overnight or by chance. It happened because I placed that bad decision behind me, made a new plan, and worked hard to achieve the success that I knew I could achieve.

Sometimes our goals will seem far away. We're like children on a car trip wondering if we'll ever arrive. But, once you've reached one goal, the second and third are easier to attain. Once you've reached a major goal and look back, the time seems short and the journey easier than it probably felt getting there.

Pay It Forward

It is easy to overlook the wisdom and knowledge of the people around you, those close to you, but try to avoid doing this. Each individual has a story and life lessons that he or she has gained along the way. The life experiences of others are great teachers. Take the time to listen, truly listen, and find the takeaways for yourself. You never know who you will meet and how they might positively impact your life.

I met my father-in-law, Lamar, a few months after Linda and I started dating. I was 20 at the time and beginning to consider what my future might become. Near Thanksgiving, Linda invited me to join her family for Thanksgiving dinner at her father's childhood home in Florida's panhandle. Coming together for Thanksgiving there was a tradition.

I agreed, albeit nervously. Then, a day or two before we left, Linda told me that I was sharing a hotel room with her dad.

Okay, I was a high school dropout, and he was a college professor. I had achieved nothing. He had achieved more than most. From my perspective, this invitation was becoming a recipe for disaster. I kept envisioning arriving and being asked how I planned to take care of his daughter. The longer I thought it over, the more fearful I grew. He was definitely going to grill me. I just knew, after our Thanksgiving trip, my relationship with Linda would end.

Fortunately, I was wrong!

Lamar Moody was the most down-to-earth, pleasant guy I had ever met. Over time, he shared his personal story with me. He grew up on the family farm during the Great Depression, and he, like myself, had wanted more from life than he had experienced during his childhood. Lamar learned to read at night by the light of a kerosene lantern and a candle. He was valedictorian of his high school class, and he became the first in his family to leave for college. He went to the University of Florida and ended up earning a doctorate in educational leadership.

Educating others became his passion and life's work. Twenty-three years of his career was spent as the head of the Department of Educational Leadership at Mississippi State University. Lamar was a great man with the skill and desire to make others feel good about themselves as individuals with purpose and ability, while at the same time, motivating them to improve.

Gardening was his hobby, and he cultivated both plants and relationships. Without fail, he and I visited a plant nursery each time we spent time together. During one of these trips, Lamar asked an employee at the nursery if John, another employee, was working that day. "Yes," the employee responded, and he went to find him for us. As we waited for John, Lamar shared that this young man had a family and was attending the local community college in hopes of providing a better life for them. When John arrived, Lamar greeted him, asked about his family, and as our conversation ended he reached into his pocket and gave him a $100 bill.

Lamar said three words as we walked away, "Pay it forward."

His granddaughter, my daughter, Lindsey, was born on his 70th birthday. Lamar passed away in 2016. I sincerely hope that the way that I live my life and the words in this book will help me pay it forward.

Faith Matters: Take Time to Contemplate God's Existence and Presence

To my youngest brother, Kevin: Your life on this earth was short, but the impact you made on your family was long and powerful. I love and miss you.

My youngest brother Kevin was born when I was 10. He was two when our family purchased a house in a nice residential area. Compared to our trailer, our new home was spacious. Now we had a real yard— and a pool. We all enjoyed our new home and neighborhood. Eric, Cathy, and I made friends, and swimming was an everyday event.

The summer following our move, my dad coached a summer baseball team on which Eric and I were playing. At age two, Kevin loved to play baseball with us. He was becoming a true sports fan.

The baseball field was within walking distance to our house, and as I was playing in the outfield during one of our games, a neighbor of ours showed up looking frantic—something was obviously wrong— and went directly to my dad in the dugout. As I watched from a distance, my dad and Eric immediately started running toward home. I left my position and ran behind, not knowing what to expect.

As I neared the street on which I lived, I saw red and blue lights shining from what seemed like dozens of ambulances, police cars, and emergency medical technicians who were all responding to a problem. Kevin had fallen into our pool, and he almost died. Though bedridden and unable to talk, my little brother lived for five years (most of it at home with us) before he passed away.

I was almost a teenager, 12, when the accident happened, and the event made me begin to truly question why we are here on earth and what our purpose is once we're gone. I arrived at a clear conclusion: God is real. He exists. And regardless of how many years we live here on earth, we have a forever home in heaven. This belief in God, for me, is a certainty. It is truth.

When I remember Kevin now, I remember the fun we had together, and I can say with confidence that he lived for a purpose. His short time with us had meaning for me, my family, and our extended family.

Many question the existence of God; I don't. But if someone were to question His existence, I ask, "Why take the chance?" Intellectually, if we believe in God and we're wrong, what comes after that? What is there to lose? We have a brief existence here.

What if the opposite is true? What if you didn't believe and then discover He's real. What then? Forever in hell isn't appealing to anyone.

Take time to contemplate God's existence. Think about it. It's too important a decision to ignore.

The issue of faith is a real one for individuals who never took the time to decide at all. Now, if someone has really thought about this and done whatever research they want to do and then decided that God doesn't exist, even though I don't agree, at least they thought about it. They made a decision. I respect that even though I disagree with their conclusion.

Many people just never decide. I can't imagine there not being a God. I don't believe earth and all of us happened by some weird coincidence. Since I believe God put us here--and I don't think there's another possible explanation—then I am required to live in a way that is pleasing to the one who put me here. For me, the risk of not believing is just too high.

God called me to make a positive difference and to be nice to people and treat them well. That isn't hard to do. It's not a difficult decision to treat others the way I would want to be treated. The reality is that atheists can do the same thing. An atheist can treat people well. We can all make the world a better place. Our reasons might be different, but the result is the same.

Family Is First

To my older brother Eric and my younger sisters Cathy and Michelle: I share many of my best memories with you. You are all wonderful people. You each have a terrific family. I am so proud of our family and each of you. I love each of you individually and our family as a whole.

In my opinion, the purpose of life is our family or core group of people. We have to make time for them. Allocating time for loved ones is especially important for those who own or run businesses. It's tempting to make work a higher priority than family life. Remember though, we have to spend time with family. Perhaps we can't schedule hours with family every day. We must attend to our responsibilities and obligations, but when the major events arrive—a game, a recital, a birthday—we must do everything we can to be there. Unless the building is burning down, I'm there.

I enjoy my work, but I work for a purpose—to spend time with family. Remember, the people close to you are important. At the end of this life, I won't say I wish I had worked more. I'll remember the times I spent with my family.

My daughter Lindsey participated in a lot of extracurricular activities while growing up. She played volleyball, was an athletic trainer, active in chorus, and she was a member of numerous academic clubs. I am happy to say that I enjoyed every game, every concert, every appearance. I was proud to sit in the stands, drive a group of players, or do whatever it took to support her activities and enjoy them myself.

Your first loyalty should be to your family. Enjoy what you do because you're going to spend a lot of time doing it, but stay focused. Give priority to your family, or core group of people, to those you love and who love you in return.

Control the Controllable

God, grant me the serenity to accept the things I cannot change, courage to change the things I can, and wisdom to know the difference. —Unknown (Serenity Prayer)

There's been some controversy about the Serenity Prayer's authorship in recent years.[2] One source states it first appeared in a 1933 article published in the Woman's Press written by Winnifred Crane Wygal. Wygal cited Reinhold Niebuhr, one of her Harvard professors, as the prayer's original author. Today it's known by most everyone and for good reason. The prayer conveys a real truth to which we can all relate. Worrying about things beyond our control is pointless. It is a waste of time and energy. It accomplishes nothing. That time should be spent working on resolving items.

One of FASTMILE's distribution centers caught fire in 2016. Warehouses are made for this. It caused about $100,000 in damage, but it could have been $2 or $3 million. One of the lightbulbs somehow exploded and fell onto a box that contained a kitchen cabinet. The flames caused the fire sprinklers throughout that section of the warehouse to douse the blaze. A total of 20 cabinets were burned, and 350 were damaged by water. It could have easily been much, much worse.

I received a phone call while the building was on fire and while I was attending an industry conference. I couldn't control it. I couldn't change it. The fire was a fluke accident, one that doesn't happen on a regular basis.

It is my hope that each person reading this book will remember this advice: Don't worry about things outside of your control. If you can't control it, then don't worry about it. Many of the points I make in the following topics relate to the Serenity Prayer for a reason.

Life Is Good

Having the opportunity to be here, to live a healthy existence, to be able to live, to learn, and to pursue professional and personal interests is a blessing. Life is good. Every day might not be great. Believing that life is good doesn't mean that all that happens to us in life is positive, or perfect, but on balance, life is a blessing and a gift to be nurtured. Most of all, life should be enjoyed.

The world around us has a lot of challenges, but I believe that majority of people are good people who desire to do the right thing for themselves and others. If your perception of others is based on the nightly six o'clock news, you probably wouldn't think so. There's a lot, especially lately, of death and terrible things happening in this world. This doesn't mean my life is still not good.

We can all too easily stay focused on the negative things that happen to us without realizing that we experience many more positive events than negative ones. If we instead keep an eye on the positives in our lives, families, friends, and good things that are happening, we easily see how good life is. Life is a blessing.

Love Yourself and Recognize Reality

The core of being a happy person is being happy with yourself and taking responsibility for your own happiness. This is another example of the Serenity Prayer's value. If something is within your control, do something about it. If it's not controllable, don't worry about it.

This means having the self-confidence to accomplish the things over which you have control is crucial. And healthy self-confidence requires self-love—the ability to look in the mirror and be happy with the whole person looking back. This is not egotistical; it's just the opposite. Loving yourself requires being honest about your strengths and weaknesses and accepting yourself as you are.

It is important to look objectively at yourself, to see both strengths and weaknesses, and not become overly self-critical. Accepting or changing weaknesses is a personal choice. If a person is willing to accept a weakness, that is fine. No one out there is perfect in all ways, and we all should be willing to accept and love ourselves completely. It is an internal process—a decision—to be happy with yourself.

There's no better teacher at this than sports. I've

played sports for a long time, both as a youth and an adult. When I served as coach of a men's softball team, I quickly learned while creating the lineup that placing myself in any position I chose would hurt the team. I had to honestly evaluate my own ability and accurately position myself to most benefit the team. We certainly wanted to win. To function as both the team's coach—the leader—and one team member simultaneously, I had to look at myself objectively, just as I did the other team members, and correctly evaluate my skills and overall ability.

Understanding your own strengths and weaknesses requires humility and giving yourself permission to be happy with who you are at the core of your being—loving self— while still working hard to improve in the areas most important to you.

Quick Hitters for Life

⚆ **Hard Work Will Make You Successful:** It is all too common for an individual to promise to take on more responsibility for the success of the company *after* the person receives a promotion or raise. This is completely backward logic. Hard work at the forefront creates success. Don't promise to work hard after something else occurs. Companies don't give raises or promotions based on what might (or might not) happen in the future. Raises or promotions are based on past accomplishments.

⚆ **Do Not Procrastinate: Do What Needs to Be Done:** Do not wait! Get done today what needs to be done, so you are ahead of your job. Then, get done early in the morning what needs to be done. Get ahead of your day before it gets ahead of you! Walt Disney said, "The way to get started is to quit talking and begin doing."

It amazes me how many people talk about doing something but never actually do it. Walt Disney knew this to be true. He knew that if people just talk about action, they are not actually doing something productive. John Wooden, the greatest basketball coach of all time, said much the same thing: "Activity does not equal Accomplishment."

☺ **Worry Twice as Much about Yourself and Half as Much about Those around You.** In business, people are *very* guilty of this. They spend too much time complaining about the person next to them who is, in their opinion, not doing their fair share of the work. Complaining about others is a loser's mentality. Worry about yourself and your success.

☺ **One Delivery at a Time:** In the delivery industry, we say, "One delivery at a time," to indicate the importance of each one. We cannot get caught up in the large number of deliveries without realizing that the aggregate occurs one single delivery and one customer at a time. This is true in everything we do. Ultimately, your life plan is accomplished one item at a time.

☺ **Details! Details! Details!** Excellence is in the details. Give attention to the details and excellence will come.

Baseball has been an important part of my life, even as far back as '78.

Linda and I began dating in 1990.

Helping Lindsey with her swing.

My family at our wedding: Eric, Michelle, Cathy,
Linda, me, Mom, and Dad (left to right)

Linda and Lindsey, the two most important ladies in my life.

Lindsey and I at a high school baseball game.

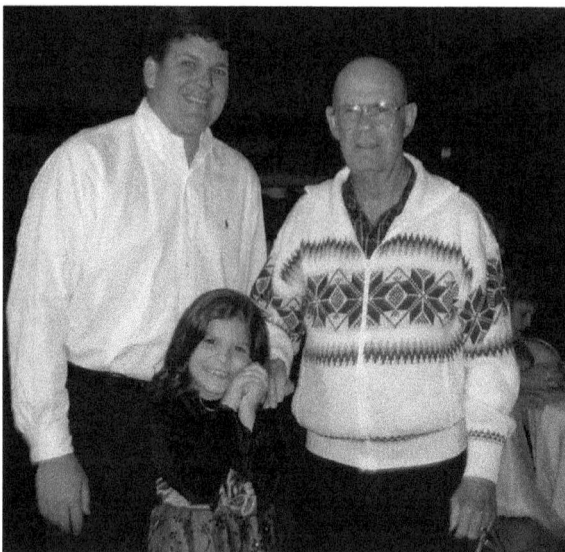

Lamar with Lindsey and me after a concert.

My family by marriage: Lance, Linda, Lindsey, Lamar, and Ruthlyn (left to right)

Our softball team after a tournament win.

Rex Theile, my business mentor and Air Traffic
Services original owner, looking good at a work party.

Part Two: On Business

Start Your Day Early

To my Grandfather, Richard Dearborn, who was perhaps the hardest working man I have ever known. He was truly part of the Greatest Generation. He worked as many jobs as he could fit into a 24-hour day to support his large family with eight children. For most of his life, he started every day at two in the morning to complete a newspaper route. After his route, he went to work at his full-time job. He had a limited education but a limitless love for his country and his family.

FASTMILE employees expect emails from me at four or five o'clock in the morning. They know I am awake and working well before the sun rises. Over the years, many people have asked me if I ever sleep. I do sleep, and I sleep well. Both rest and relaxation are important to perform at our peak capabilities.

Waking up early gives me a head start on the day, and it helps me remain in control of commitments and obligations. I begin each day with a to-do list that I hope to complete before eight in the morning. I am a busy person with a lot of responsibilities, and it helps to take care of many of the day's agenda items early. I'm not alone; there are many articles and blogs out today covering the habits of successful people. Without fail, starting the day early makes the list.

Start your day early and get done what you need to do, then the rest of the day is yours to enjoy. I'm the president of the company. I can start work at any time I choose, but I want to finish each day early to have free time each afternoon for activities that I enjoy.

After waking up early for so many years, I am disciplined and time-oriented. I don't need to set an alarm clock to wake up at a set time. Instead, I tell myself what time I want to wake up, and that is when I wake up. I have not needed an alarm clock in more than 25 years.

Never Stop Improving Yourself

Keep improving yourself. Don't ever stop learning. As people grow older they often begin to believe they've heard or seen everything. That's just not true. There is always something new to learn, something we can improve upon in our own lives.

It is important to step back, take a good, honest look at ourselves, and ask: What do I do well? What do I not do well? By doing this we attach to ourselves a life scoreboard. We keep our own score and learn from our strengths and weaknesses—our wins and losses. Then, to improve, we set goals to improve the weaknesses that matter most and take the necessary steps to be successful in those areas.

Each year, I use the week between Christmas and the New Year to evaluate the past year and to look ahead. During the week, I set goals for myself and my business. These are not resolutions; I set actual goals. Then, I develop a method to quantify each goal to help me easily measure progress. On the first week of each month, I review my progress toward reaching each set goal. I ask: Am I working toward accomplishing it? Do I need to change course?

If it's a financial goal, I check to see where we

are, then I keep moving down my list. There may be 20 goals listed each year. I don't accomplish all of them. Sometimes I move goals ahead to the next year.

Measuring non-quantifiable goals can be challenging. By their very definition, you cannot assign numbers to measure your progress. For me, these qualitative goals are typically items that I need to improve to make myself a better leader or person.

One year, I decided one of my weaknesses was not saying thank you to employees. To become better at expressing gratitude for a job well done, I decided to write a thank you note and give a gift card to one employee each month who offered exemplary service or went over and beyond to do their job well. I placed a monthly reminder on my calendar to keep myself on track. At the first of the month, if my reminder arrived before I had given the thank you and gift card, I made sure to do it. This turned a non-quantifiable goal into a quantifiable one, and today I'm better at recognizing effort and saying thank you.

Image Is Important

Rex Theile, Air Traffic Services' original owner, taught me a lot about business. The most valuable lesson was taught by his business style. He was and is a bottom-line guy. With Rex, fluff doesn't matter. The most important question to ask in any business transaction is "How much money am I making?" Profit is the bottom line. Rex was happy with a small company that employed a handful of people. He was happy if he came in each day and could chat while getting the work done. Rex and I worked well together.

When I decided to return to college, he was against it. At first, he really didn't want me to begin a new future track, but eventually, he accepted that college was in my best interest. "Just get it done," he advised. "Don't drag it out because you're working. It's not about fun. Just finish." That is what I did.

While I was in college and working fewer hours, I wanted a raise. I believed I deserved a raise, so I asked Rex for one. He thought about it and came back to me with a decision, "No." His decision took into account that I was still in school, leaving early for classes, and not in the office as many hours as I once was.

I knew if I wanted a raise, I would have to come up with some new way to prove that I deserved one. There wasn't a lot I could do work-wise to improve, so I determined to find another way to stand out. The very next day, I started wearing a tie, and I continued to wear one for many years.

In our industry, when not working with outside customers, some employees wear shorts to work. Previously, I always wore dress slacks and a polo shirt. I thought the added dress shirt and tie would help Rex see that I was serious about my role at work, and that my job was more important than simply a paycheck. I believed that a 20-year-old wearing a tie would give him a different impression of me and my commitment to the company.

I was asking for about $50 extra each week, not a lot. But I needed the money, and I thought I was worth it.

It's so easy to give up when we don't have control over circumstances. The challenge in these instances is to ask yourself: "Can I control it?" and "Is there something I can do differently to achieve the outcome I envision?" It is all too easy to blame others for your result. Our challenge as people is to accept responsibility for our outcome, and then have the discipline to create our desired result.

Six months later, Rex came in to see me and said he thought it was time I received the raise. He gave me the $50 each week and a little more. Even though he did not give me the raise because of how I chose to present myself, I am certain it made a difference.

Organize, Organize, Organize

To my mother-in-law, Ruthlyn Moody, whose home, heart, and life were the perfect balance of strength, warmth, and elegance. She was the definition of southern hospitality. I love and miss her.

Working as a teen at Red Lobster was a terrific learning experience. My role there as kitchen manager helped me learn the importance of organization early in life. At 16, I was responsible for food preparation and keeping the kitchen clean and organized. My overall duty, in my opinion, was to meet customers' expectations. I believed customers wanted their food prepared properly and quickly, so I directed my team to emphasize food preparation.

From my managers' viewpoints, the kitchen functioned great. Guests were repeatedly satisfied with both the quality and timing of their menu choices, but they pointed out its chaotic appearance. To management and visitors walking through the kitchen, we lacked the visual neatness that they expected. This lack of neatness implied disorganization. I failed to meet one of my two main responsibilities.

This experience taught me that keeping things organized demonstrates to those observing—whether they are visiting for two seconds, two minutes, or a longer time—that we have what we are doing under control. Organization is also important for employees and those who use the space daily. Keeping space clean and organized helps us take greater pride in our work.

Skip forward a few decades. Today, on my office desk at all times is one small notepad with a blue pen and red pen. That's it. Nothing else. My desk looks organized. In reality, it is organized. I keep my space orderly beyond what is visible to onlookers because it's time effective—it's efficient—to quickly find what I need.

For each delivery we make, the customer signs a paper release verifying receipt. Every day, we collect thousands of delivery receipts. Over a year, this number grows to millions of pieces of paper that need to be organized in some way that ensures each can be easily located. We should be able to find, and can find, each document within minutes. Otherwise, asking the customer to sign the receipt is wasted time.

It doesn't take a whole lot of extra time to be organized on the front end, so it's organized in the back end. Organization is imperative. It's good to both appear organized and to be organized. Simply stated: organization saves time and energy.

Control Your Emotions

It's not often that someone yells at me, but when it does happen, I hope to retain mutual respect and find a peaceful resolution. Recently, a decision I made greatly upset a valued and respected long-time employee. This person entered my office and began—in a raised voice—verbalizing their disagreement. In more blunt terms, he was yelling at me. The emotion in this context indicated passion for FASTMILE, and while I don't mind zeal and fervor—disrespect is unacceptable. This outburst was bordering on disrespect.

I remained silent and calmly listened until the employee's anger was exhausted and the complaint was voiced. I appreciated their honesty. To this person's credit, their views and complaints never escalated to disrespect. The argument's focus remained on the decision itself and its effects on this employee. He did not focus his anger at me as the person who made the decision. It did not become a personal attack.

Once the yelling ended, I explained why I made the decision that I had made. He disagreed, but we both accepted the other's position and ended with a smile, a handshake, and respect for each other.

Teams grow through differences. Diversity can provide creative solutions to complex problems, but we must always remain in control of our emotions and respect our differences.

The reality is that words and behavior cannot cause anger unless we give another person power over ourselves. We each have the ability to interpret messages and situations. I could have allowed my employee to anger me. I could have yelled back. I could have escalated the situation to a conclusion that was poor for everyone. Instead, I choose to respond calmly and rationally.

Giving in to anger never leaves a positive result. In the end, nothing is accomplished. It forces a fight or flight response. The other party will either fight back or stand in the corner. If I yell, they're going to respond with similar aggression. That response is not likely to lead to a successful remedy to the situation. Clearly, there is a problem. We need to solve the problem and not lose our cool with one another.

Control your emotions or they will control you. Keep the situation—whatever it may be—calm. Lead rationally, not by emotions. Refuse to be led by emotions, up today, down tomorrow, and always respect the differences of others even if you don't agree.

Trust but Verify

Ronald Reagan used the phrase "trust but verify" in 1987 when he signed the arms agreement with then Russian President Mikhail Gorbachev.[3] It is as true today as it was then. Not only dangerous situations but day-to-day tasks require verification of completion.

Trust but verify is a core business principle that builds accountability.

It happens all the time. Someone says, "I took care of it," when in reality, they didn't. Through the years, I've learned to trust employees, and at the same time, verify the task is actually completed. Lack of follow-through can present problems.

Recently a FASTMILE customer visited one of my facilities. The customer brought a team of six people from various parts of the United States to review items as they arrived at our facility for storage and delivery. This particular customer manufactures household items, and they wanted to compare the items' condition from the point of leaving the manufacturing plant to their condition upon arrival at our facility. Their quality inspection team had to be present at our facility to inspect the items as soon as they were unloaded to make an accurate assessment. For my customer, quality control was important, and my team planned their arrival for weeks. We worked out a special location to unload this specific truck, and we set up an inspection area for them. Everything was prepared. The afternoon before their arrival, we confirmed our meeting at seven o'clock the next morning.

Following my "Trust but verify" advice, I called my warehouse supervisor at five-thirty the next morning to verify the truck's arrival. He confirmed its arrival. I asked him to verify that the truck was in the proper location. Again, the plan was unfolding perfectly. Then I asked him to verify that our team was ready to unload the trailer when the customer arrived. To my shock, he said: "They just started unloading it." It was five-thirty, not seven o'clock! They were supposed to wait for the customer's arrival. At this point, only two of 200 pieces had been unloaded. We quickly stopped their unloading. Thankfully, I verified our plan was being executed or something we had planned for weeks would have been pointless. Instead, the inspection process happened as planned, and my customer never knew anything had gone wrong.

I trust my team. They do a great job. However, I also verify that tasks and projects are finished properly. In this example, by verifying our plan was progressing properly, I was able to avert a disastrous outcome, and instead the plan happened perfectly from our customer's perspective.

If I ask, "Hey, did you handle this?" they know a quick "Yes" will get me off their back for the moment. If I don't verify that it was done properly, to the standards that I expect, then over time they will know that they can just give me any answer. My calendar is filled with items to follow up on to verify completion.

Don't assume anything is complete. Over time it's understood that I will check. Being upfront with your boss is difficult sometimes, but a direct approach is better than a platitude. It's better to speak up immediately than to wait until the sky falls—when it's obvious that you didn't do what was expected. It's better to tell the truth—not simply what someone wants to hear—because together we can move forward to a resolution.

Teamwork

To my softball friends and teammates: We won a lot of games together, but it was never about winning. It was about our families. It was about each other. It was about a team. We relived some of our "glory days" and had a great time in the process.

I love sports. I've always felt that participating in sports is one of the best teaching tools for life. I love that you are one player on a team of 10, 20, or 30 people. To be part of a team, there has to be an honest awareness of your own ability. To know that you are not as good as some players and better than others, and that is okay. I love that it takes people with different abilities coming together to make a team. We're not all wide receivers, not all quarterbacks, and not all offensive linemen. We all have different strengths, weaknesses, body types, and the like. That is just life.

Companies, too, are like this. Each employee has different motivations and skills. All types are needed: those who enjoy physical work, those who like to lead, and those who like administrative tasks. My job is to place people in the position that maximizes their talents. Jerry Rice is probably the best receiver in the history of the NFL. If he played offensive line, he would not have played football past high school. In my company, I have to make sure every person is in the best position for our company's success.

I personally believe that people struggle with the fact that some people are not as good as themselves at certain tasks. They think, *I could have done that faster*, or, *I wouldn't have done it that way*, but that is just reality. Each person is unique. In basketball, most of a team's points are scored by few players. That doesn't mean that the players scoring the most should look down at the rest of the team. All players are needed, and everyone plays at his or her ability level. If someone on the team has the attitude that they have done their part and stops giving his or her best, now expecting everyone else to do as much or more, that is an attitude of failure. We must each give 100 percent.

Imagine a basketball player complaining to his team members "I have scored 10 points, so I am not shooting again until someone else scores." The player's coach would be incredulous; that is a ridiculous remark, and it represents what one employee does when they choose to belittle another team member because they feel that person is not doing their fair share.

Giving participation medals to five-, six-, or seven-year-old children is fine, but by age eight, I don't agree with the practice. In sports, it's crucial to teach players that failure is part of the real world. You're going to strike out. Failure is critical to future success. I wasn't always the best player, but sports were essential to learning those lessons.

When the scoreboard is turned on, children learn that failure is part of the real world. The lessons that happen in sports are critical. By keeping score, we know the lessons from that game in both victory and defeat.

Just the same, we cannot turn off the scoreboard of our life; it is always on. The question is whether or not you will look at it honestly and use it for your benefit.

Deal with Reality (It Is What It Is)

Purposefully notice the conversations around you. Inevitably, at some point, someone will say, "It is what it is." The cliché, used by star athletes, top coaches, politicians, movie stars, and everyday people, is generally a confirmation of the reality of a situation, not an escape from it. Often a coach or player will use the saying after a bad game to confirm the play or result wasn't desired or expected, to accept accountability, and to move on.

March 2008 was a turning point for me and FASTMILE. After careful consideration of current delivery industry trends and opportunities combined with our company's current and projected five-year financial performance, I was convinced I had to begin to expand the size of my facility to have the necessary infrastructure to handle our projected growth.

I signed a lease for a spacious warehouse in Orlando. This commitment was HUGE—one larger than any I had previously made. FASTMILE was now obligated for millions of dollars in debt. It was the right decision for us and made at the right time, so I believed.

It was a dream building. The offices were brand

new and built to our specifications, and the warehouse space was in pristine condition. On Labor Day weekend of 2008, we moved in. Then, two weeks later, on September 15, Lehman Brothers collapsed, which created an avalanche of business failures and the worst recession in 80 years.

I planned. I made the right decision based on known facts. My team did everything right. Unfortunately, a series of disastrous external events caused my company to start losing business. Late 2008 was a horrible time for FASTMILE and many other companies. As a company, we had the choice to either complain and get upset over what was happening or accept the reality of the situation. We made a new plan and survived. In fact, we thrived. In mid-2009, FASTMILE expanded to other locations and states.

"It is what it is" highlights the importance of facing the reality of any situation; however, it doesn't imply that we can't plan for and produce something better in the future. It's not an excuse for bad performance or behavior. Remember, the reality of where you are may not be where you want to be, but don't dream up reality. It is what it is.

The reality of where you are is only your current situation. All things change. If it's bad, fix it, but don't pretend it's not bad. Being honest with yourself and others about the reality of your current situation makes it much easier to plan for a different future outcome.

I'm the Hardest Working 84-Year-Old You'll Ever Meet

In the early '90s, an elderly man stopped by the office to apply for a job. Back in those days, our application was a basic one-page information sheet, and when someone came in looking for employment, they would sit down at the table in the lobby and complete it right then. If I happened to be present, I would pay attention to how the person engaged the front-desk employee because typically that is how they would engage customers when making deliveries. I also noticed how long it took for the prospective employee to finish the application.

This man walked in, asked for an application, and left, taking it with him. I thought it was an odd thing to do.

Then, a week later he returned with the application completed and gave it to the front-desk person. The employee brought it back to my office and said, "The guy is back."

He had used a typewriter to complete the application. Never had anyone done this.

I noticed his name, Bill, and brought him back to my office to talk to him, fully intending to tell him there were no current openings. He walked slowly and looked advanced in age. That was the way this was going. I planned a straightforward approach. We reached my office, and as we were making small talk, he says, "I know you see my date of birth."

"Yes, yes, it's here on the application," I responded.

"I'm the hardest working 84-year-old you'll ever meet."

I said the first thing that came to mind, "Bill, I think you're the only working 84-year-old I've ever met."

We sat and chatted for a couple of minutes more, but his open, direct comment about his age convinced me that he was worth a try. Bill started working with us a couple of days later, and he worked with us for seven years. He truly was the hardest working 84-year-old I have ever met. One day, while at work, he had a heart attack and died. No one saw it coming. Everyone at the office loved Bill, and we felt the void his absence left behind.

A few days later, I went to his funeral. I didn't expect his pastor to mention his courier job at all. After all, he spent 84 years of his life working somewhere else before he came to work with us. He had a large family with many children and grandchildren, and he was active in his church. People filled every pew. I was there to pay respect to Bill's life; I didn't know his family or friends, so I found an empty space to sit in the back.

When the pastor began eulogizing Bill's life, I was shocked. He spent 15 minutes—more than half of his message—sharing about how Bill would often share with his friends the details of what he had delivered, where he had gone, and who he had seen along the way. I learned how much Bill loved his job at his funeral.

Wanting to express my sorrow for her loss, at the end of the service, I approached Bill's widow. She asked my name and then, hearing it, broke into the biggest smile. She grabbed my neck and gave me the nicest hug, all while expressing Bill's appreciation for both me and FASTMILE.

Bill's funeral profoundly affected me. That afternoon, I learned an essential lesson. People give of themselves when they work, and we, as leaders, have a responsibility to take care of them. Their work—a large part of their lives—is centered around the same professional goal as my own. We have different roles in the company, but we want the same outcome.

Complaining Is for Losers;
Deal with It or Quit

If I were to call some of my longest-tenured drivers right now, those who have been delivering since '91 or '92, they would have the same complaints they made in the '90s. Okay, we started that contract in the mid-'80s. It's now 20 years later. It is obvious that the job can't change. The issue is uncontrollable, so either deal with it or quit. So much in life can be outside our control, but some things are controllable. If freezing temperatures bother you, don't move to Alaska.

Complaining injects negativity into the person complaining. Any pattern of thinking repeated enough becomes a habit, and these habits shape our lives. Negative and positive thoughts both grow. They're seeds we cultivate. If a person allows negativity to dominate, over time a limited worldview and self-defeating inner voice is created. Being positive doesn't mean that everything is good. Be realistic. Make it your objective to view any situation from both viewpoints—make a pro and con list if you want—and move forward based on the best option.

If You're Going to Do Something, Do It Well

To my FASTMILE team: Everyone who works within our company makes me proud on a daily basis. Together, we work hard with the singular purpose of providing our customers outstanding service. I appreciate and value what you do every day.

People, especially young people without a lot of experience, will accept a job—any decent job—to earn a paycheck, knowing the job is not permanent. The type of job is unimportant; be the best at it that you can be. For example, accepting a job as a bartender might not be ideal if you don't enjoy being around people who are drinking, but a bad attitude won't help. If you're a bartender, be the best.

We were searching for a new customer service representative a few years ago. Typically, we would place an advertisement for them, receive resumes, conduct interviews, and choose a candidate. However, this time was different; a current manager mentioned that he knew someone who might be a good fit for the position. I learned that this person helped my manager regularly at a fast food drive-through.

I was amazed that someone at a drive-through would make such an impression on our manager. Many drive-through employees don't care about their job or the quality of their work. This person was clearly exceptional. We hired her, and she did a great job for a number of years before leaving for an even better opportunity. She did her job at a drive-through so well that it became a launching pad for her career.

Who knows what job comes next? Your current position may lead to a great opportunity in the future. You may land a great job from the people you meet along the way. If you're moping around, making sure everyone knows you don't like your job, those opportunities are likely to pass you by.

Freight on the Dock

Adding new customers while retaining old ones promotes steady, manageable growth. For FASTMILE, this means we take great care to realistically plan for new accounts. It is imperative that we have both a plan and the resources—both human and material—to execute deliveries for all of our customers successfully. So, in 2009, when I received a call from a potential new client, an online retailer who expected 100 orders a day, my team worked hard to develop a workable storage and delivery solution for them.

The client was detailed and forthcoming with the product and delivery information we needed to implement a strategy to fulfill their orders perfectly. We invested numerous hours preparing for a successful launch. Only, on launch day, no orders arrived. Concerned, I picked up the phone and gave them a call. "It's starting a little slow," I was told. "The orders will be here tomorrow." The next day was a repeat of the first. In the end, we fulfilled a total of three orders.

Though it felt as if all of our planning was a

waste of time, in reality, it wasn't. Our plan was impeccable. The problem was that I did not verify the potential orders were real. I should have qualified the customer more accurately.

On the surface this seems a business-only issue, but in life, too, we often create plans with others or independently set a goal for something we want. Ultimately, action must follow planning to make the plan real and the goal achievable. The plan's outcome has to become tangible. It cannot simply exist in our mind or desire.

Let Others Gossip for You

Let's start with a fundamental truth: If you want to keep something to yourself, keep it to yourself. If you tell anyone, assume you have told everyone.

Don't try to prevent gossip. It happens. People talk. Instead, ask how gossip can be used to your advantage to achieve a positive outcome. I find it is best to manage gossip by becoming the news source. Don't hide or shy away from either good or bad news. Get in front of it, and be present and truthful.

In baseball, players "get in front of the ball." Players anticipate where a ground ball is going—instead of where it is—and they get there first. The decision of where to throw the ball to get an out or prevent a run is made before the ball is in the glove. In the same way, when dealing with news, decide how to frame the message in the way you want to present it. You should never change the content of the message. You have to be honest. However, the frame around the message will be put there by you or someone else. If you don't frame it, others will. I try to frame every important message in order to place myself in front of the situation.

Once you've thought through the message and how to frame it to others, get the information out quickly. For example, if we lose an account at work, I make sure to get the information out first, so it is presented the right way. In this way, I know employees have received accurate information, and the message is from my perspective.

If the news is positive, sometimes it can be shared better by one person telling another person and so on. It's better if one person tells the next, and the next. In that way, the gossip train can be used to an advantage. If I know something is coming, I'll tell one or two people, and within minutes everyone knows.

When dealing with negative news, I find it best to tell managers together first at a prearranged time. Immediately after the meeting, I email all company employees. Doing this prevents gossip from growing, and it helps combat miscommunication.

Effective communication requires message management. When all employees are included, it is easier to control the content and tone of the news and ensure the details are correct.

How You Leave a Relationship Is as Important as How You Enter It

A new relationship, whether business or personal, is exhilarating. It is exciting to start something new. For some people, they are constantly searching for a new project, a new customer, a new friend, even a new personal relationship. The excitement of something new can act like a drug. Every relationship evolves and changes. It cannot possibly remain new forever, and almost every business and personal relationship will end at some point. The way we end the relationship can have a longer lasting impact than how we started it.

About 10 years ago, we had a large customer who stopped using our services. It was upsetting. We had provided this client exemplary service and didn't deserve to lose the account. We wanted to tell the them our thoughts and how upset we were that they decided to leave. It would have felt good to pull resources away from the account during its transition to another company. We would have saved money by removing expensive people away from this account. However, we did not do any of those things. We decided that leaving a relationship in a positive way is just as important as entering the relationship in a positive way.

We gave this customer tip-top service until the day they stopped using our delivery services. Seven months later, they called us back and wanted to resume working together. This call would have never occurred had we not left the relationship in a positive way. Ten years later, they are still a great customer.

When We Lose It's My Fault; When We Win It's Their Credit

As a business leader and coach, I take the blame for losses and give credit for wins. I create the overall plan and place the people in positions that I believe give us the best opportunity for success. If we lose, it is because I had the wrong plan or placed people in positions unsuited to their strengths. It is my fault! If we win, we won because those people worked hard, executed the plan, and it led to the desired outcome. They get the credit!

We had an account in 2016 that was not working properly. From the outset, this account functioned differently than disclosed before we took on the new responsibilities. The customer, a home-goods manufacturer, presented us a straightforward delivery model. We were to receive items from their manufacturing plant, then schedule and make delivery to the purchaser.

We accomplish this same process thousands of times each day, and we believed this account to be a perfect fit for our operation. Unfortunately, it was not. Repeatedly, the customer changed the orders and the ordering process—even as the items were in transit to their intended destination. The complexities caused repeated failures and frustration for all the employees working with this account. We struggled for a few months to work through the challenges until I realized we couldn't meet their needs, and I made the difficult decision to end the relationship.

Upset, the customer immediately blamed my salesperson for misleading them. I stopped them mid-sentence. "It is my fault," I said. "I accepted your account, and I am to blame." I would never allow my employee to take blame.

Make sure to credit the group for wins. Neither self-promotion nor blame of one person in a team environment is productive. If one person, especially the coach or team leader, focuses on either self-promotion or the abasement of one member, the other team members will follow along. Your leadership attributes—respect, humility, honesty, kindness, etc.—are important. Be a leader you would want to have, and your team will respect and emulate your character and methods. Teach others how to live and care for others by your genuine example of appreciating the contributions of everyone on your team.

Grow Wisely

To Rex Theile, my business mentor, who taught me to always watch the bottom line. He taught me to manage people. He taught me to give employees responsibility and authority in equal measure. His teachings and guidance made me a better leader and businessman.

Imagine I am holding two notebooks in front of you, and you have a decision to make. You can either earn $10 to deliver the blue notebook or $100 to deliver the red one. Which delivery job will you accept? Will it be the blue or the red notebook? Ninety-nine percent of people look at me like I am stupid and say, "The red one."

The reality is that this is a trick question. How? I never provided the address to which the notebooks are being delivered. The red notebook is going to Alaska, and your next-door neighbor is expecting delivery of the blue notebook. Now, I ask again, which notebook do you want to deliver?

Believe it or not, it's common for companies to have revenue of $100 million, $500 million, or even $2 billion and lose money. In my judgment, this happens because they didn't grow wisely. Often companies grow their business completely with sales without paying attention to the bottom line. Leadership neglects to keep watch on profit margin. Sell, sell, sell is the mantra, while the cost of making the sale is overlooked.

A sales-only approach does not achieve growth. Growth is achieved through increased profit, and profit is determined by sales and the expenses incurred to produce those sales.

Once you have a plan in place, account for cost by carefully including all expenses, and make sure to include a line for savings. It may take a while to reach a goal, but delayed gratification is worth the effort.

Good Times Aren't Here Forever;
Plan for Lean Times

Throughout most of the last century, Lehman Brothers was one of the largest investment banks. In business since 1852, the bank had survived recessions, the Great Depression, two World Wars, and countless good and bad times. In 2007, they reported income of $19.3 billion. In September 2008, they were in bankruptcy. How did a company go from $19 billion in sales to bankruptcy in nine months?[4] Economists and historians will analyze and debate this for years. I will not attempt that here. However, I will point out that they clearly did not prepare for bad times. According to the Wall Street Journal, Lehman Brothers paid its top 50 employees over $600 million in 2007. The *lowest* salary of the top 50 employees was $8.2 million. One employee was paid $99.8 million over a three-year period.

Amongst other mistakes, Lehman Brothers believed that the good times of the 2000s would last forever. They failed to plan for a downturn. The company was unprepared for the 2008 collapse. As a result, their entire business went into bankruptcy and the financial world together with every investor suffered untold losses.

In business and life, expect financial ups and downs. Repeatedly, I've watched business leaders, for whatever reason, spend excessively when times are good. They give everyone a raise or expand the size or scope of business. While that may be good, good times aren't staying forever. Raises are good, yes, but it is better to make frugal financial decisions when times are good to create the financial backup that is needed when times are bad.

We saw this happen to many good businesses besides Lehman Brothers during the '08 collapse. Small and large companies that had good financial earnings for 10 to 20 years were out of business following an economically bad six months. The decisions made during good times carried forward. If the companies affected had saved the surplus profits—refrained from giving lavish bonuses, extras, and the like—they might still be in business today.

It is imperative to make wise, frugal decisions when times were good. Don't look at only right now, look two or three years forward, and make decisions accordingly. Success requires setting goals—both qualitative and quantitative—and plans to reach them. Being frugal means paying cash for large and small purchases. When times are good, it's easy to purchase on credit. Business owners and individuals look at the immediate cash flow and think, 'It's okay to buy on credit. I can do this. I'll pay $200 a month, or $1000 a month.' What if you lose an account, your job, or something else happens? When times are good, it is best to pay cash outright for purchases. Don't buy on credit. In order to attain your goals and plans, consistently save for lean times and large purchases.

Time Is a Non-Renewable Resource; Use It Wisely

Time is finite. It's a non-renewable resource. We are each given 24 hours in a day, no more and no less. No one can create more hours in a day. You can earn more money and make more friends; it is possible to create an abundance of things, but once the day is over, it can't be relived.

The important factor related to time is how to allocate or manage it to accomplish the most possible each day. Effective time management requires a plan. There are many methods to manage time, and all of them require keeping a calendar to plan effectively. Workdays, days off, and holidays can be planned, though it is important to leave time for rest and unplanned activities.

Set goals and create milestones toward them in your calendar. Get in the habit of including your tasks, and take the time to document each day's objectives. If a productive work day is ahead, start with a to-do list.

As you know, I suggest an early start because play time is important, too. The habit of keeping a calendar is an effective way to work toward your daily, monthly, and yearly goals. Remember: each day that you plan is a day closer to achieving your goals.

Short-Term Solutions Don't Solve Long-Term Problems

Problem solving requires forward thinking and sometimes sacrifice. We make decisions every day, some more important than others, but when we are working toward a goal with a plan in place, our decision-making process should align with these. Employing good decision-making strategies cultivates tomorrow's growth and success.

Making decisions that benefit the team and company over the long term, not only today, is a constant battle. It often happens in business. A great example is the need to fill an open position that requires a specific set of skills and experience.

In 2015, we had an open dispatch position. A manager came to me and recommended that we ask a previous employee to return to work with us to fill the role. I knew this employee and remembered their skill set didn't include attention to detail, and this caused problems on numerous occasions. This person's skills were not right for the position or our company in the past, yet now I was being asked to bring them back. When I asked why we should ask this person to return, the manager replied that it was easier to fill the role with someone who needed minimal training. I disagreed because I felt this hire would create a long-term problem with a short-term solution.

Instead of hiring the former employee, we started looking for a new hire. It took a while, but after poring over numerous resumes, we found someone who seemed to fit the position perfectly. She came to work with us and immediately made us a better company. Over the long term, she took on additional responsibilities and even developed internal cross-communication channels between departments that both improved the customer experience and our administrative functions.

We can easily focus on short-term needs and seek quick resolutions. In this scenario, it's filling a position quickly or waiting to find the right person, but daily we make many business and life choices that help us right now only or help us reach our long-term goals. It is best to keep your end goal top of mind when making decisions that impact your progress. This way, your decisions will most likely help you reach your destination quicker because you're taking the most direct route.

Live Life to Win; Don't Be Afraid of Losing

To Lindsey, my daughter: You are my legacy. The world has a lot to offer if you are willing to work hard and sacrifice to achieve your goals. It is your time! You can do this! Play the game of life to win and help others along the way! I love you.

In life, there are winners and losers. We should do everything we can to win, to achieve our goals. We shouldn't go through life afraid of losing. People who live life afraid of losing live fearing what might go wrong. The potential for failure becomes the central focus, and the resulting anxiety can cause distraction and immobility. Those who live life fearing failure, I don't believe, can ever win. To win in life, to achieve a goal, you must create a success strategy, implement that strategy, and execute it. As changes develop along the way, you adapt. It's important not to live fearing what might happen.

I was asked to help coach a high school baseball team in 2014, and I almost turned down the opportunity. I was going to say no even though I am passionate about working with young people and helping them achieve their goals. Several close personal friends work and coach at this high school, and my daughter Lindsey attended the school and was one of their student athletic trainers. The position appeared to align perfectly with my skills, personal life, and desire to help.

It was an honor to be asked, but fear of failure kept me from immediately accepting.

Baseball has been an important part of my life since T-ball. My dad coached my little league teams until I was 13, and I assumed I would one day do the same. I planned to have both a daughter and a son. God blessed me with a truly wonderful daughter, but we never had a son.

Lindsey loves sports, too, and over the years we have developed a great relationship. I enjoy the time we spend together more than words can express. I love her unconditionally.

Still, attending baseball games over the years was an emotional struggle for me. I wasn't coaching my son, and remaining at the field for an entire game was difficult. It is the smell. Baseball has a unique smell— one of the best smells in the world. Unfortunately, the smell brought thoughts of unrealized expectations. My first thought when asked to help coach was, *No way. How can I say yes? How will I deal with the emotions at practice every day?*

I shared my decision to turn down the offer with Linda and Lindsey. Lindsey changed my mind.

"Daddy, please do it," she said, trying to encourage me. "I'll be the team's trainer, and we can do it together."

Lindsey reminded me of a critical life lesson: Play to win; don't be afraid to lose. I was afraid of losing. Lindsey was playing to win.

If you are going to play to win at life, it is necessary to take risks. Success comes after you have exposed yourself to potential failure. It is all too easy to never expose yourself and to stay in a safe zone. As an outfielder in baseball, sometimes you have to dive for the ball to make a critical catch and help your team win. If you dive and make the catch, you will help put your team on the path to victory. However, if you dive and miss the ball, the other team's chance of winning greatly increases. Therefore, the outfielder has to trust their training, preparation, and skill to dive at exactly the right time and at the right angle. To win games, you have to dive sometimes; you have to take a chance. To win at life, you have to trust your training, preparation, and skill to make the right decisions at precisely the right moment.

I said yes to coaching the team, and it has been one of the best decisions of my life. Lindsey and I have spent a lot of time working together, and I have been blessed to work with many young men who have enriched my life.

Every dream and goal you have for your life will most likely not come to fruition. Every person will experience unrealized hopes, setbacks, reversals, and even upheavals sometimes—life changes. Build resilience within yourself by purposefully practicing a positive mindset—especially in difficult times—and keep an open heart and help others. Don't expect to receive everything you want or work toward in this life. Truthfully, sometimes we all lose, but if you play to win, you will win. And when you look back at the losses, or unrealized hopes, you will see that it was your wins that defined you and the unrealized hopes perhaps became your greatest areas of growth.

Every business decision can be bad. Every decision a coach or player makes in a game can go wrong. Sometimes we lose, but that doesn't mean we don't decide. Decisions are based on what we believe is best given the information we have, and we expect it will work. We don't make decisions based on the chance it won't work because some decisions won't work even though everything told us it should.

I treasure my time on the field with the team. We work together to improve our team and individual baseball skills. I hope that I have made a difference in their lives.

Make the Lives of Others Easier by Working for Their Benefit

This, I believe, is perhaps the hardest thing for people in positions of leadership to do. Most business leaders expect the employees reporting to them to work for the benefit of the leader or company. They expect those who work "underneath" them to continuously work for the benefit of the leader or owner. I don't believe that is a successful mindset. I believe, as the owner, it is my job to work for the benefit of the people who work with me. Notice I don't say "for me" because I don't think that way. The people who work with me, we work as a team.

If I make their life better, if I notice they are struggling to finish a particular task in a timely manner or if they're just not grasping how to accomplish an assignment, it is my job to help them through it successfully. Sometimes this might mean doing the job for them. Sometimes it might be by showing them another way to accomplish the same goal. Ultimately, I am working for their benefit. If I work for their advantage, by natural progression, they will work for the company's advantage. Working for another's gain creates a culture of working together and is a perfect example of what happens in a well-functioning team.

Years ago, an employee was struggling with completing an administrative responsibility on time. I truly believed that the task should take only two hours, but for this employee, it was a six-hour effort. I asked them to share why the task took so much time to finish, and then I struggled with the explanation I received. To better understand the process, I decided to take on the responsibility myself. Within an hour, the task was done. The actual time required supported my belief that two hours was sufficient. When I shared the method and process I used with her, she was thankful. I used a different approach—one she had not considered previously. After she started using the new process, finishing within an hour or two was easy. We were all winners!

On a baseball team, all players are not equal. Some players hit better, some run faster, and some score more than other players, but everyone works for the benefit of the team. If the shortstop can cover a little more area than the third baseman, then the shortstop is working for the benefit of the third baseman when he makes a play that the third baseman couldn't make. In this way, the team is better and winning is within reach. In turn, the third baseman might be a better hitter than the shortstop, so he works to make the team better by doing what he does well. The best teams, whether it be a sports or business team, or a family for that matter, work for the good of the people around them. They perceive themselves as a team and work for what is best for the group, even if it is not best for the individual.

People in leadership positions find the concept and action of working for another's benefit difficult to do because they don't necessarily perceive the value of working for the benefit of someone at a lower corporate level than themselves. But, indeed, it is important for leaders to lead by example, to exemplify team effort by working for the benefit of other team members as necessary. Leaders should strive to make the lives of team members easier. The result is a well-functioning team.

It's important to continue to look outside of ourselves and work for the good of others. We should always ask ourselves: (1) How can I make a difference in the lives of those in our company? and (2) How do I make a positive difference in the lives of people with whom I come into contact?

Saying No Is Taking the Easy Way Out

No is the easiest word in the English language to say. When you tell someone no, the conversation ends. There's nothing else to do—nowhere else to go.

"Can you make a delivery before two o'clock this afternoon?"

"No."

That's it. It's done. The conversation is over. The sale is lost. When someone hears the word no they naturally resist it and move on to someone who will tell them yes.

We should challenge ourselves to say yes to see if we can make it happen. Before telling someone no, we should ask ourselves, "How can I do this? Could I accomplish it?" By considering taking on the task or event, we challenge ourselves to accomplish something difficult.

If we honestly challenge ourselves, and the answer is still no, then we should provide another option when possible. If a customer asks if we can make a delivery by two in the afternoon and we simply cannot make that happen, we could offer another option such as "We can make it by two thirty," and then work to make the delivery on time.

Self-challenge is not easy. It is all too easy to tell ourselves that we don't have time or resources or any other excuse. We can justify almost anything in our own mind. In many instances, we are lying to ourselves, and unless we are willing to challenge our internal voice, we will accept the lie.

Every Yard Has Bugs

"The grass is greener on the other side" is certainly a familiar saying to all of us, and the adage is especially true in a business environment. It's easy for a person to examine their job and see its inherent faults. To be clear, every job has faults, less than ideal tasks or responsibilities.

Though I'm not the first, I feel this way about my neighbor's lawn. It seems that whenever I glance next door, my neighbor is outside gardening. He is constantly mowing, fertilizing, weeding, trimming hedges, or just doing something to make his yard look great. Then, I look at my yard and see only the areas that need attention. I see the "bugs" in my yard, and my less-than-perfect lawn encourages me to compare the two. I begin to think that his lawn is perfect, and mine is an eye sore.

In reality, my lawn looks fine, but I want it to be perfect. I am more judgmental of my own lawn than my neighbor's. I see the beauty of his lawn while noticing first the flaws of my own.

This is exactly what we do in life and work. We see the imperfections—the bugs—in our own environment and the perfection in another one.

Often, we look at other job possibilities and assume it's perfect somewhere else. Many people work for a year at a job and then move on; they're looking for a greener yard. They spend 15 or 20 years with 10 different jobs and never develop a sense of home or stability that comes with a long-term position.

Loyalty between the employee and employer doesn't develop when a person sees only the challenges in their current job responsibilities and seeks a "bug-free" position elsewhere.

I'm a loyal person. I strongly believe it is important to give your current situation every opportunity to improve. Do what you can to improve it. Don't simply look at the bugs and start over elsewhere. Work to get rid of the faults. Don't expect perfection elsewhere. Bugs are everywhere.

Loyalty Is a Two-Way Street

To my good friend Bobby Guthrie, who is the most loyal friend and person whom I have ever met. You are always there for a friendly talk, and you have an amazing ability to make people feel better about themselves after being around you.

Too often business owners demand loyalty from employees without offering the same in return. As employers, we demand employees to make work their priority, and often work must be first priority. Employees are expected to come through on every task or responsibility asked of them, and if we've chosen the right employees, they will come through every time. In recognition of performance or effort, employees might hear "Thanks!" or "Great job."

Appreciation does not constitute loyalty. Loyalty toward employees means standing with them when times are rough—when a bad decision has an impact, or when challenging life circumstances arise. Often, too often in my opinion, employers fire someone for making a mistake or a bad work choice regardless of the countless past times that same person successfully came through for the company. Loyalty should be a two-way street, both employer and employee should work for the best interest of the other.

I support employees in decision making. Everyone can make a wrong decision, including myself. I support my employees. I chose them. I placed them in their positions. They are a part of my team.

Poor decisions can usually be overcome. It concerns me more if an employee isn't confident enough in their job or position to make a normal decision regarding a work situation at all. Decision making is a shared responsibility at FASTMILE. Every employee wants to make a positive difference, and without the freedom and responsibility that comes with decision making, they can't. It is important to create a work environment and develop job responsibilities that provide the opportunity for each employee to experience the satisfaction of personal growth and the knowledge of knowing their personal contributions contribute to the overall success of the company.

We all know that people are imperfect. We all make mistakes sometimes. Bad decisions and difficult life situations will occur. Regardless, I believe that I can't demand loyalty from employees if I'm not willing to give it in return.

Certainly, there are times that I have to decide I can no longer work with an employee. It does mean that loyalty goes both ways. If you are on my team, I will support you as long as you are making decisions consistent with our team vision and goal. You can't have a workforce that works for you effectively without team loyalty.

Organizational Circles

The traditional top-down, triangular-shaped organizational chart implies that the chief executive is more important than everyone else on the team. This concept should be rejected. It implies that somehow I am more important that everyone else on the team.

FASTMILE's organizational chart is a series of circles. The center circle is the president and it moves outward, not by importance, but by the flow of information and decisions. Everyone works together.

The circular pattern highlights a decision-making mindset. Sometimes I will make the final decision, but I am not at the top of the triangle. Everyone has an equally important role to play in the company with shared responsibility, and we all work as a team.

Quickly Answer Your Emails, Voicemails, and Texts

Imagine talking with someone face-to-face and they simply stop answering you but continue to look at you. You ask them a question only to be ignored. No answer. You ask again. Again, no answer. If this happened in a face-to-face conversation, you would consider that person rude and would likely not talk with them again. Similarly, when someone communicates with you by email or text, respond to them! Respond quickly. Even if the answer is that you are busy, and you will follow up with them in more detail later, that is fine. However, always treat them electronically with the same courtesy you would have face-to-face.

Fire People in Person

When I took over FASTMILE in the mid to late '90s, Jeanne, Rex's existing administrative assistant, continued in her role and became my administrative person. Jeanne and I were two different types of people, and we never clicked. Both our work styles and personalities were opposite. Eventually, I fired her, but I didn't handle it well.

Before firing her, I should have met with her to offer a list of areas in which her performance needed improvement, but I didn't. My vision for FASTMILE was different than the previous owner's, and I should have given her an opportunity to embrace the company's new focus. I wasn't fair to her in that regard, and I regretted how I handled the situation.

Firing a person changes their self-perception. Today, from a managerial standpoint, if someone is at the point of being fired for performance issues, it is my policy to be honest and share with the employee the areas that must improve to continue working together. I owe them the opportunity to improve. Sometimes FASTMILE is not the right company, or the job responsibilities are not the right fit for the employee.

Firing someone doesn't mean that I am always right, but it is sometimes an unfortunate decision that has to be made. It is almost like breaking up with someone, but I must do what I believe to be best for the company overall.

When faced with firing someone, or if you at some point find yourself in a role that isn't best suited to your skills and talents, remember that ultimately personal success comes down to direct, open communication. Specific job responsibilities help both the employer and employee know and understand the employee and his or her role. If you are in a managerial role and someone consistently performs poorly, schedule a meeting to openly discuss the specific responsibilities or expectations that need improvement. Then, if performance doesn't improve and you have to fire the person, always do it in person. You are going to shatter that person's life, and they deserve to be able to look at you and say what they want to say. They have earned that right.

If you find yourself unable to adequately perform an expected task or role at work, respectfully share your challenges with your employer. The desired outcome is for both the employer and the employee to grow. Many successful people have been fired, and when they look back they see that being fired forced them to develop their strengths, and the experience pushed them to become more successful.

If You Swim to Shore, Walk onto Land

This is dedicated to one of the best operations persons in the world: Raymond Millan. Raymond works harder and solves more issues than any person I have ever known. He always finishes the job, walks onto land, and then makes the shore cleaner and more organized than it was when he arrived.

A customer called two days ago and said, "I really need a favor. I desperately need this order delivered tomorrow morning as soon as the recipient opens its business. Can you do it?"

We accepted the job and set everything up. We readied the delivery and dispatched a driver. He left our facility and arrived at the delivery address on time. He made the delivery on time. We did it. We made a commitment to our customer, formed a plan, and made it happen!

So, what's the problem?

The problem is that we never communicated to our customer that we successfully made the delivery. We didn't finish the job. We didn't tell them it was done. We didn't take credit for our hard work. We did the hard work, but we failed at the easiest part.

This is a constant challenge to everyone. If you are going to do 99 percent of the job, do the last 1 percent. The hard part is behind you. Now, finish it.

In my company we call this "Walk onto land." We face challenges that seem like we are in the middle of a lake and our boat just got a hole in it. We have to swim to safety. We work hard to get out of the situation. In essence, we swim to shore. Then, after finally solving the issue, we take a breath and relax. We are finally past the issue. However, did we really fully complete the issue or did we just get close enough to shore to think we are done? Did we finish the job? Did we walk onto land?

Success Does Not
Happen by Luck

Sometimes, I am driving down the road with a series of traffic lights in front of me, and as I approach, every light is green. When this happens, I was lucky. I was lucky to be driving at the perfect speed at the perfect time.

Success is not lucky. Success is creating a solid plan and executing it. Success takes hard work, dedication, flexibility, determination, and a never-ending drive to *win*! I refuse to discount success by calling it lucky. Each person who has created and accomplished a plan is to be commended and complimented.

Winning the lottery is luck. Winning at life is the culmination of a well-executed plan.

Quick Hitters for Business

☺ **Learn the Personalities of Your Employees and Customers**

We all have different personalities and motivations. This is true for employees, customers, family members, and everyone with whom we interact. It is our responsibility to learn about each person and work with them in a way that motivates THEM. It is not about us. Our goal is to get them to respond to our wishes.

☺ **Accept Responsibility for Solving the Issues You Receive**

If an issue finds your desk, it is your issue to handle. I refuse to be in charge of a company where people simply push their responsibility off to someone else. As consumers, we too often get caught in the "large company loop" where one person simply passes us to another person who then passes us to another person. In the end, nothing is accomplished. At FASTMILE, if an issue reaches an employee's desk, it is their responsibility to find a resolution and communicate that to the inquirer or customer.

☺ Professionalism Is Our Constant Goal

You never know when someone is watching. Always handle yourself in a professional manner.

☺ Never Get Comfortable with Success

Simply because we were successful last week does not mean we will be successful next week.

☺ If It Were Always Fun, We Would Not Call It Work

Work is just that—work It is not always fun. On many occasions you will have tasks that you don't want to do. Who cares if you want to do this particular task or not; it needs to be done, so get it done.

☺ Recognize the Big Picture but Focus on the Daily Details to Bring the Picture Together

As managers, we need to understand the big picture, the overall company goal, and know we are working toward achieving our goal. However, our goal is accomplished by focusing on the daily tasks and details for which we are responsible.

☺ Treat Everyone the Way We Want to Be Treated

Of course, the Golden Rule is crucial to success. We should treat our customers and our coworkers the way we want to be treated as customers and as coworkers.

☺ Managers Create the Atmosphere, Tone, and Culture for the Entire Company

As company managers, we have many responsibilities. At the top of that list is setting the tone for the entire company. The way we carry ourselves, what we say, and how we say it defines who the company is.

☺ If It Were Easy, Anyone Could Do It

A business exists because it is providing goods or services better than its competitors. This means that sometimes it is going to be hard and involve hard work. Recognize that being hard is part of being better.

☺ Be Passionate!

"Passion" is a big word with a big meaning. It indicates depth. Passion reveals desire and love. If you are passionate about something, you are willing to invoke your best efforts to achieve success. As a company, we should be passionate about our work. We should never accept anything less than our best.

As individuals, we have a responsibility to be passionate about life. Life must be lived with depth and love. Our passion needs to bring forward a never-ending desire to WIN at life!

☺ Maybe It Is You

When a problem develops, ask: "Did this happen to me, or because of me?" Too many times individuals look at a situation and blame someone other than themselves. A person committed to winning in life will always look within, will ask themselves if they caused the situation at hand. Blaming others will never fix a problem. It is critical to take a good look in the mirror if you want an issue resolved.

☺ Treat Your Employees the Way You Want Your Customers Treated

I cringe when I see a leader yell or talk down to an employee. When a leader does that, they are teaching that employee how to speak to others. Therefore, when a leader yells at an employee, that leader should expect the employee to yell at a customer.

☺ Create a Positive "Life Cycle": Always Work for Our Customers and Their Customers.

In the logistics industry, we are providing services to our customers. If we can provide a service that is good enough for our customer to add additional customers, then we are creating the need for our customer to use our services more often. In reality, we created our own growth by providing quality service. This "life cycle" is a self-fulfilling and positive growth strategy.

Improve Every Situation because You Are a Part of It

Every day we go through life, we encounter dozens of people in multiple situations. I strongly believe that we each have a responsibility—yes, a responsibility—to make every person and every situation better because we are there. When paying for groceries, share an encouraging word with the cashier. At work, make sure to say, "Good job" to a coworker. If a server is behind at a restaurant, and slow to take care of us, be the person to make their day better by being patient and waiting a few extra minutes.

As a leader in my business, one of my core responsibilities is to improve the lives of everyone in my company and the lives of our customers. I also make it a priority to make every project better because I was part of it.

This mindset is critical. If we make this a priority for ourselves every day, we will improve both our part of the world and ourselves. Our individual lives will be better because of the effort.

As this approach becomes part of our life, the end of our lives will be met with the satisfaction that this world was improved because we were in it.

A Challenge: Be a Rock, Not a Feather

To Michelle Williamson: It has been a lifelong goal of mine to create a book from my experiences and the lessons this life has taught me. Your professionalism, attention to detail, and passion for writing has made this process thought provoking, challenging, and enjoyable. I so very much appreciate everything you have done to make this goal a reality.

A feather tossed into the air will land wherever the conditions take it. If the feather is lucky enough to catch a strong gust of wind, it might travel far distances. If there is no wind, it will land in the same place it started.

I've met many people during my lifetime, and most of them live lives shaped by the conditions surrounding them, like the feather.

Now, consider a rock. It's strong. It has a solid core and is heavy enough to plot its own path. When directed and thrown, the rock cuts through external conditions to reach its desired destination on its own.

I challenge you to be the exception. Be the rock: steady, solid enough to create your own path through life. Make your own course. Plan your life; you can achieve your dreams.

Notes

1. "Michael Jordan's Quotes That Will Immediately Boost Your Confidence," Inc., accessed December 16, 2016, http://www.inc.com/benjamin-p-hardy/23-michael-jordan-quotes-that-will-immediately-boost-your-confidence.html.
2. "Serenity Prayer Origin," Huffington Post, accessed April 24, 2016, http://www.huffingtonpost.com/2014/05/15/serenity-prayer-origin_n_5331924.html.
3. "Trust but Verify an Untrustworthy Political Phrase," The Washington Post, accessed December 16, 2016, https://goo.gl/oEK2Ab.
4. "Lehman Brothers Collapse," Investopedia, accessed April 24, 2016, http://www.investopedia.com/articles/economics/09/lehman-brothers-collapse.asp.

www.ingramcontent.com/pod-product-compliance
Lightning Source LLC
Chambersburg PA
CBHW060614200326
41521CB00007B/769